AMAZING SNAKES

Contents

Written by John Townsend

Mrs Carding

The Amazing Snake!

a sidewinder snake

Have you noticed that you don't need very fast legs to be a hero? Not if you are a snake!

Snakes have magnificent powers.

Let's find out what they are.

Snake Senses

Living animals give off heat.

Many snakes can 'see' heat in the dark. A fancy central organ in their head senses living prey at night. It can tell the difference between a dead rat and a sleeping mouse.

A snake can quickly sense and catch a mouse in the dark.

Ears inside my head help me balance.

A snake has no ears on its face, but it can still sense noises. Snakes pick up sound waves in the air or on the ground.

This is how snakes pick up smells in the air.

Smooth Snakes

Snakes have an amazing power to keep their skin smooth.
They chuck it away!

A few times each year, snakes shed their old skin and slip away looking like new.

Snake Defence

Some snakes have a priceless power. They sink their fangs into an enemy's skin. Chomp!

This snake's bite could kill up to 100 humans or 250 thousand mice.

The poison is so deadly that it kills with one bite!

Some snakes can shoot poison with spot-on aim if they are attacked. A spitting cobra will raise its head and hiss.

Then it will spray poison a short distance into the air. Its poison hits its enemy's face like burning acid.

Hero – or Not?

BUT ... a deadly cobra is no match for a mongoose. Sometimes a mongoose will circle round the snake to tease it.

Then it will pounce, kill and eat
the snake.

So just think ... even a snake is
wise to be nice to a mongoose!

Glossary

balance	to keep steady
fangs	large, sharp teeth
mongoose	a fast-moving mammal with a long tail, about the size of a ferret or stoat
organ	part of a living thing, such as an eye or ear
prey	an animal that is hunted for food
sense	to become alerted to things by using any of the five senses: sight, smell, hearing, touch, taste
sound waves	wave-like flow of air that carries sound